# Hail Mary

Originally published as *L'Ave Maria*

English translation by Bret Thoman


Library of Congress Cataloging-in-Publication Number: 2013942098

ISBN 978-0-8091-6768-5 (hardcover)
ISBN 978-1-58768-326-8 (e-book)

Published in English by Paulist Press
997 Macarthur Boulevard
Mahwah, New Jersey 07430

www.paulistpress.com

Printed and bound in the
United States of America
by Versa Press, East Peoria, IL
August 2013

# Hail Mary

EXPLAINED BY
Ermes Ronchi

ILLUSTRATED BY
Tommaso D'Incalci

Paulist Press
New York / Mahwah, NJ

# WHY THE HAIL MARY?

The Hail Mary is, without a doubt, the most often recited prayer to Mary—by people alone, in their homes, and in their communities. It is the most beloved and most well-known for many reasons.

The Hail Mary was inspired by God in the first part and born of our life in the second part. It allows us to breathe with both lungs of every prayer: praise and petition.

The oldest part—that of praise—is drawn directly from the Gospel of Luke. It comes from the words that God put in the mouth of the angel Gabriel on the day of the Annunciation, when Mary, amazed, received God within her. It also comes from Elizabeth on the day of their happy visitation, when Mary would joyfully sing out her Canticle.

The biblical part of the Hail Mary offers a short, but strong, summary of the Nazarene girl's entire story. It tells us what she is before God (*Rejoice: you are full of grace, God is with you*), and before other people (*blessed are you among women, and blessed is the fruit of your womb*).

The second part—that of petition—was formed slowly over many centuries. It took its current form as late as AD 1500. It includes very old teachings of the Church. For example, in AD 431, Mary was given the name Mother of God at the Council of Ephesus. It also reflects our need for the presence of a friend as we walk with God each day (*pray for us now*), until the end of our life (*and at the hour of our death*), when we pass into heaven.

The Hail Mary is, then, a prayer that comes from God and people. It is made up of words that came down from heaven and rose up from the earth. These words take us by the hand and accompany us inside the sacred story. This story is of Mary, but it is also our own, because we are all called to become mothers of our God, who always desires to come into the world. And it is up to us to help him be born again in our heart, in our house, in our journey.

Because the world is a vast Bethlehem.

# Hail Mary

*And an angel came to her and said, "Hail Mary, full of grace, the Lord is with you."*

“Hail” is the first word.

This is not a simple greeting, as in “Hi” or “Hello.” Instead, the angel brings a wish that is almost like a command, and means: “Rejoice, be glad, be happy.”

This word is like a beautiful musical note,
a nice-smelling aroma, or a tasty and rare flavor
that we search for each and every day:
it is joy.

The angel does not say,
“Get on your knees, pray, or do this or that.”

But he simply says,
“Open yourself to joy,” as a door opens up to the sunlight.

God comes close to us and caresses us,

God comes and holds us in his arms.

He comes with a promise of happiness.

Because of this, we listen to him and follow him.

# Full of grace

The second word of the angel contains the secret of joy:
Mary, God has fallen in love with you.
You stole his heart
and he filled you with light.

You now have a new name: "Beloved forever."
Softly, freely,
without regrets, you are beloved.
And your name is also our name:
Good or not so good, everyone is *Beloved forever*.
Young or old, we are all filled with heaven.

Like Mary, I, too,
am like a jar that overflows with the life of God,
I, too, am a vase that is filled with
the softness of heaven.
I, too, am beloved forever.

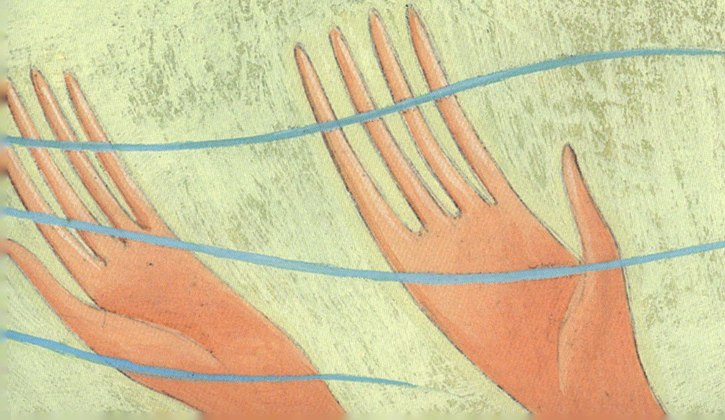

The Lord is with thee

The third word of the angel says:
Mary, you are like the house where people and their God embrace.
You are where the journey of two beggars comes to an end:
One is of love, and is a person;
the other is of love, and is God.

God's name is: "I am with you."
Wherever you go, every step you take,
whenever you fall and are hurt,
when you get back up and smile again,
I shall be with you, all your days,
until the end of days.

The God who never rejects anyone is with you,
the one who will never abandon you,
the one who rejoices when he is with you.
He is with you, as close as your heart, as close as your breath.
He is like your core being, and you are like his core being.

## Blessed art thou amongst women

*And Elizabeth was filled with the Holy Spirit and exclaimed with a loud cry, "Blessed are you among women, and blessed is the fruit of your womb.*

Mary and Elizabeth hugged in an embrace
and words came forth from the union of their love.
The first is like music that surrounds all mothers of the world
because they are all blessed:
"Blessed are you among women."

On Mary, still today, the blessing from heaven
comes down to cover every fragment and every part and piece
of Mary that is throughout the world
and bears the name woman
as a pure force of goodness
that makes life spring up in all its forms.
Woman is a blessing of God for the world.

I wish to receive the first word of Elizabeth in my heart:
To *bless* the Lord, life, nature,
the sun, and the blue sky, brother fire, and sister water.

And also: blessed are you, Mom,
blessed are you, Dad.
And all you who love me.
God blesses me with your presence,
May God bless you with my presence.

And blessed is the fruit of thy womb, Jesus.

Mary, earth of God
you received a seed, you gave back its fruit.
He grew from you, he danced within you,
you nourished him with milk, with dreams and hugs.
In everything, he is the same as we,
Yet, he is the most beautiful and blessed thing that ever
happened to the world.
He was for us what spring is for flowers.
He told us about God as someone tells a love story,
he made poor people the princes of his kingdom,
he made children the elders of his house.
He gave everything, he did not even keep his own body for
himself:
"Take, eat."
He forgave the people who killed him.
And God raised him up so that it would be clear
that whoever lives like him shall live forever.

I bless Jesus, the fruit of your womb, Mary, and the fruit of
heaven.
May every child that is born
be blessed for the earth,
a unique word that God said
and will never again repeat.

## Holy Mary

*The first part is praise, the second petition.*
*But the prayer never ends in Mary;*
*instead, she is like a road sign,*
*a direction sign that sends us onward.*

She is holy, because she came from the hands of God:
From his creation, God knew how to extract
a look that does not lose the innocence of its sparkle,
a hand unable to strike,
a word that does not know how to harm,
a heart that cannot hate,
a face that reflects the beauty of God.

Holy, because she loved:
because of the free and joyous love she gave her Joseph,
her baby, the bride and groom at Cana,
and to John when darkness overcame the land.

Holy, because she believed:
at the tree of the cross,
before the empty tomb,
in the upper room of wind and fire.

Holy, because she is loved by God:
She emptied herself out to him and he filled her,
she is hope for us all to become saints,
because we are all loved.

# Mother of God

Mother of man,
you have two lives. You live if your son lives,
and you would have wished to die in his place.
Mother of Jesus,
who is God and man, our own flesh filled with heaven.
Mother of the crucified God,
where love is consumed and life flows.
Mother of the God with us, who journeys along our roads.
You slow your steps to our speed,
and wait for us, smiling, because you know that we
easily tire.

One night—among the scent of milk and pastors—
you brought a son into the world.
In Nazareth, you taught him how to love and to smile,
to embrace and to be happy, to pray and to choose.
Mother, you who teach how to live,
let us come to you as to our own teacher of life.
Your calling is our own: teach us to be mothers.
We, too, are mothers of God, helping him to come to earth
once again.
We, too, are mothers of man, caring for other lives
with our own life.

## Pray for us sinners

We pray to you,
you pray for us,
just as you prayed in Cana for the bride and groom.
You, who see first when the joy of our houses comes to
 an end,
protect our loved ones.

Pray for us to the Lord,
so that he lowers himself and pays attention to us
and joins his breath with our breath.
So that not even a single cry is lost, not a single tear.
So that he is connected with us, in our going and in our
 staying,
so that he gives us what we need to be happy,
but never alone.

Pray for us, that his forgiveness comes upon us—
for that which kills, for that which causes suffering,
for that which does not know how to bloom,
for having loved little and badly,
—his forgiveness in time and eternity.

# Now

Now, when the cry of the orphan rises up,
the fear of the person cast away,
the sadness of the one who is alone.
Now, when violence is king
and the self-respect of man and woman is humiliated.
In this moment and in every moment,
when the innocent victim cries out,
Mary, pray to the Lord for us.

So that signs of hope blossom forth,
so that men and women live the Gospel
and make the earth more beautiful.
Pray and give thanks to the Lord with us.

You, sister, who go before our long caravan,
teach us to walk in the world like you,
caring for life with a free and strong heart,
while serving God with honesty, and our brothers and
sisters gently.

# And at the hour of our death

Pray for us, when evening comes,
at the end of the day, at the end of life.
Pray for us and for those we love.

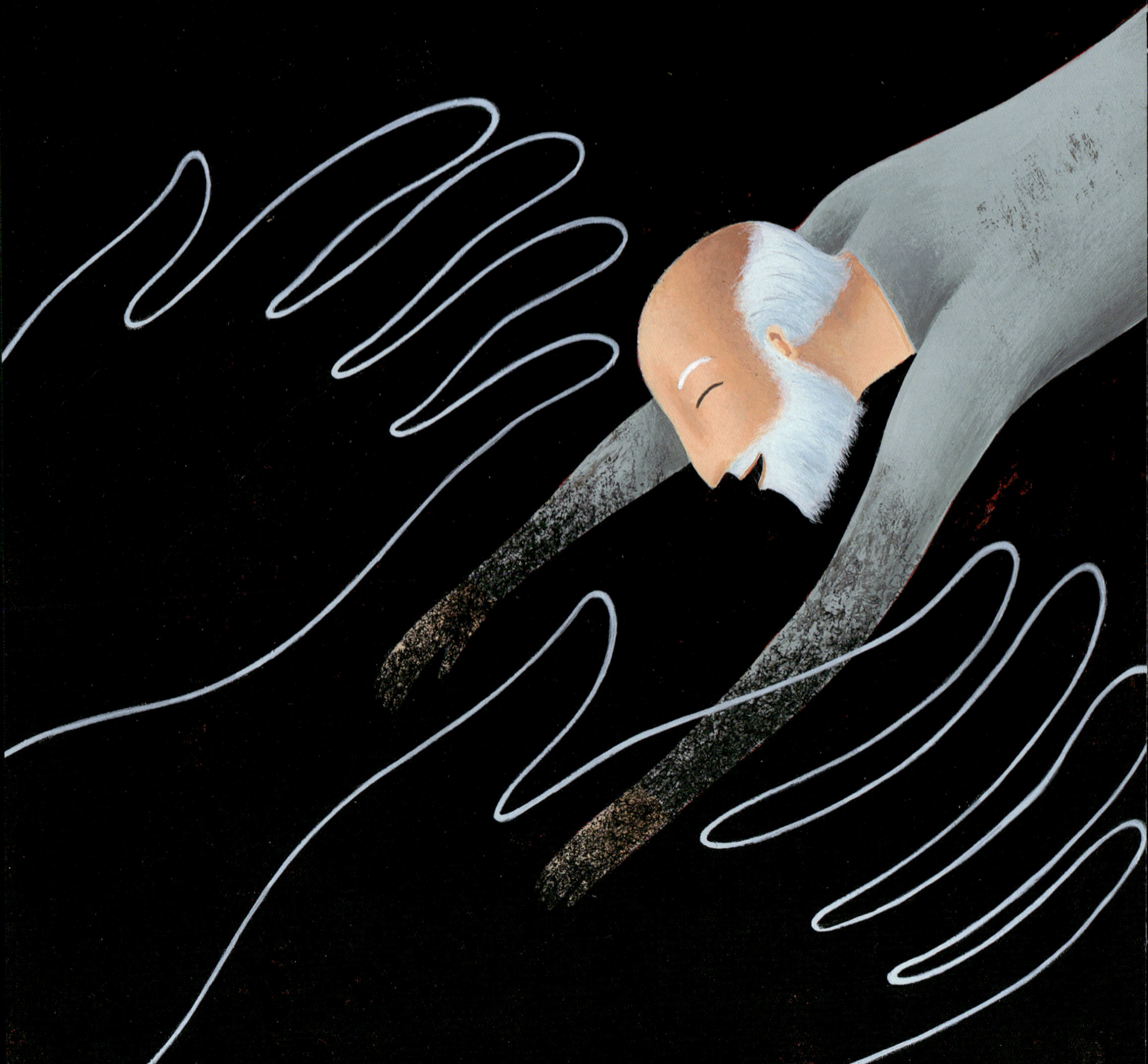

Pray so that death becomes like our sister,
so that our faith is like that of children,
who leap up into the sky with trust
knowing that they will fall into the hands of those who love them.

And after a brief darkness, it will be like coming out once again into the sunlight,
like when separated friends meet again.
And we shall feel a gaze of warm light on our faces,
and a voice saying:
"Come, dear, now you will no longer be harmed."

Pray for us to your Son
who fills even the streets of death with life.
Pray for us
at the hour of our death,
and of our life.

## TOMMASO D'INCALCI

Tommaso D'Incalci was born in Torino, Italy. Since childhood, he has always loved to draw and doodle on whatever was around him. After graduating in set design from the Academy of Fine Arts in his native city and some experience working in drama and television set painting, he decided to transform his main hobby—children's illustration—into his work. So he competed in several illustration contests, and in 2005, he was chosen for the exhibition of illustrators in a children's book fair in Bologna with a book project on Genesis. He has collaborated and continues to collaborate with numerous Italian and foreign publishers.

He currently lives and works in Lugo di Romagna, a city near Ravenna in the Emilia-Romagna region of Italy.

## ERMES MARIA RONCHI

Ermes Maria Ronchi is a priest and theologian in the Order of the Servants of Mary (Servites). He had many jobs before becoming a priest, including a stint as a street sweeper in Canada. Such experiences taught him that all life has great value. Today, he works with several newspapers, including *Avvenire* (a popular Catholic weekly publication in Italy) and he leads the commentary on the Gospel for the Italian television program, *A sua immagine (In his image)*, on the major Italian network, Rai Uno.

This is the first time he has narrated a spiritual story for children. In doing so, he chose Mary, someone very dear to him.